WHEN MOM DIES

A Daughter's Unique Guide to Help Heal Grieving Hearts Today

BY DACKEYIA Q. STERLING

KeyQuest
PUBLISHING

WWW.WHENMOMDIES.COM

PUBLISHED BY KEY QUEST PUBLISHING
Copyright © 2014 by Dackeyia Q. Sterling
Publication Design: Dackeyia Q. Sterling

ISBN-13: 978-1500990794
ISBN-10: 1500990795
Self-Help / Death, Grief, Bereavement
Inspiration

To obtain excerpts, options and other permission(s),
submit written requests to:
Permissions, Key Quest Publishing,
P.O. Box 1623, Bowie, MD 20716.
Send emails to: CEO@EntertainmentPower.com.

Dedication

***

*This book is dedicated with love to the memory
of my dear Mother,
Eloise Easterling Fortenberry.*

*Thank you, Mom!
Not a day goes by that we don't miss you.*

***

*To Del, Taylor, Daddy, Shime, Jay,
Antracia and Lecia,
this book is also dedicated especially to you.*

***

*For those coping with the loss of your Mother,
hold on!
You will make it through!*

Special Note:

***

Gardenias were my Mother's favorite flower.
Remember / Mom's Love / Forever

Table of Contents

Preface

I have been compelled to compassion.

I have written this book to help any and everyone who has lost their beloved Mother. My wounds are still fresh. A million memories and moments flood my mind. In fact, I cried until 2 am this morning thinking about my Mother not seeing my brother's son who was recently born.

Part biography, with a few details about my Mom included as part of my tribute to her, and part inspiration for you and I, ***When Mom Dies*** delivers love, strength and compassion for our hearts -- for years to come.

Stay encouraged. The sun will shine again. The overwhelming grief and sorrow felt when Mom dies is a painful, life-changing experience that takes time and love to heal.

As you read these pages, I believe you will gain

strength to celebrate your Mom's life, legacy and honor your Mother in ways you never imagined. Your Mom lived, birthed you and loved you *so greatly* that the world will *never* be the same again.

Think about that. That's powerful, good news!

<u>*Introduction*</u>

The Day My Life Changed Forever

Like many of you reading this book, my Mother was my very best friend. Her name was Eloise Easterling Fortenberry. Mom was a beautiful, tall, country-born girl from Mississippi who lived in California most of her life. She was a devoted Mother, grandmother and a powerhouse matriarch who loved us well. She passed away on September 5, 2013, at the tender age of 62 -- while holding my hand.

For one year, my mind refused to believe what I had seen. Literally, I could NOT believe that MY Mother was gone. I couldn't believe that I witnessed Mom's passing. Couldn't believe that our mother-daughter relationship was over. That all the great times, great food, vacations, lifelong advice, shopping sprees, financial figuring outs, rich, rich, rich family love, even sickness and hospital stays...was over.

Couldn't believe that my brothers and I had to sit on that front row with our family at church for her funeral. Just couldn't believe it.

I discovered in the days immediately following my Mom's passing that there were several books dealing with the stages of grief, but I couldn't find anything to speak to the reality that I was living.

When Mom Dies is a practical and unique book from a daughter's point of view of the techniques, tips, resources and advice that I have LIVED through since my dear Mother's passing. It was very therapeutic and cathartic writing this book - - better than writing in a journal. Creating and compiling helpful lists and quick ideas to help comfort grieving hearts gave voice and form to the most traumatic experience some will ever face.

I had NO idea what to do that day, nor the many, many days after my Mom's passing...until...after a few days, as one day turned into two and two into 10 and so on, here we are, with a book guaranteed to give _you_ hope for the days ahead.

I am sharing these words with you in the hope

that these short chapters give you more strength, useful tips, encouragement and advice as you navigate your next steps.

<u>When Mom Dies</u> is a quick-read filled with love and uplifting intentions.

DACKEYIA Q. STERLING

<u>Chapter 1</u>

What To Do When Mom Dies?

From the moment my Mother passed away, to the slow-motioned minutes immediately following -- as the doctors and nurses started offering their condolences, hugging me and my daughter, many with tears in their eyes -- to the time that the chaplain left us alone in my Mother's hospital room, all was noticeably silent.

Mom was really, really gone and I was tasked with informing everyone.

As I looked at her deceased body laying peacefully still, in retrospect, I realize that the magnitude, finality and reality of my Mother's death hadn't actually sunk in. Still, with cell phone in hand, I tried hard to focus through the tears on how to start speed-dialing -- making the hard calls that my/our

Mom had just passed away.

After I called my two brothers in California, I called my husband who was working in D.C. that day. Then, I called my Dad, my Mother's six siblings, Mom's best friend Linda and our great Aunt Clota Mae -- all in California. Then, I called the funeral director from our church, a nice, professional business owner named Deacon Horton -- who I had called a few months earlier in anticipation of this day.

Imagine this shell-shocked daughter standing there, having absolutely NO idea what to do next! Mom birthed me, loved me, clothed me, fed me, taught me, counseled me, prayed for me, stood by me, molded me, blessed me, lovingly devoted her life to me and my brothers...and now we had to say goodbye.

It was simply terrible.

As my six-year old daughter watched me, I gathered my Mom's personal belongings from the hospital room. One last kiss on Mom's forehead. My first grader and I prayed, then took our quiet walk to the elevator, hand-in-hand, down the hospital corridors, to the elevator, to the parking lot, to our black Mazda CX7 SUV. We stopped by McDonald's for her favorite sundae, topped with M & M's of course.

Our drive home was quiet and painful. When I looked in the rear-view mirror, tears streaked my daughter's face like fresh rain on a windowpane and she was now asleep. I reached back and held onto her left leg for much of the drive home.

Opening the door to the house and NOT hearing Mom say her usual "Hey family!" made us stop in our tracks. In an instant, we knew and could feel for the first time that our lives were forever changed. Before moving another step, we stood in the kitchen for a pause, listening to the silence.

That was the first day.

In the months since, I have cried, prayed, struggled, waited, pushed and pressed my way to today. So many days were indescribably painful and difficult. Everyone's grieving process may be different, but I have learned that losing your Mother is a life-changing, game-changing experience that I wouldn't wish on anyone.

Chapter 2
What Else Did I Do?

Once family and close friends were called, I posted my Mom's passing on my Facebook wall. Once her obituary hit our local newspaper a few days later, condolence calls, cards, emails and gifts started flooding in. One of my friends from college named Sonja mailed me a small box of Sees Candy. So, one day, I sat on the couch while everyone was gone and I ate the entire box -- crying, reminiscing and commiserating over what had just transpired.

"Sorry for your loss," "Sincere condolences, love and prayers," and "May God comfort your heart" were common themes I heard and read.

Friends I hadn't spoken to in years called, texted and showed up. I spoke to some on the days I could speak without boo-hooing. Others I let go straight to voicemail. Still, I was grateful for them all. All that love in a short span of time was strengthening in ways I couldn't recognize, define or feel at the time.

After planning Mom's funeral service with my brothers, I searched the web for a book to help me with next steps. I couldn't find one dealing with a daughter's point of view so I settled on a book on Amazon that caught my attention entitled _The Funeral Is Just the Beginning: Everything You Need to Do When a Loved One Dies_ by Amy Levine. I read most of it and followed it to the letter. I went to the bank and courthouse to handle final details. It was my turn to endure the worst pain of my life and I discovered that crying in private is one thing...but crying in public places was a terrible new experience.

Every day, my heart was literally hurting -- kinda felt like it was skipping a beat and doing cartwheels at times. I had to breathe deeply and repeatedly remind myself to "BREATHE!" just to calm down.

Decades of the richest mother-daughter love I will ever know was over. To save and rescue myself from additional pain and what felt like my own certain, impending death, I reluctantly drove to my doctor's office for a checkup. My heart was hurting so bad that I had to make sure I wasn't having a heart attack.

Gratefully, I was physically fine. My mid-day crying sessions, late-afternoon moping and middle-of-the-night panic attacks were all part of the grieving "process" I heard so many talk about.

I called the advice nurse at Kaiser Permanente and looked online for grief counselors after my high school friend Amy recommended a grief support network called GriefShare.org. I never attended any support meetings -- but I did read some good death and dying material on various websites. My prayer partner Bobette in L.A. shared other great resources with me. And my childhood and college friends Antracia, Keyandra, Lori and Larry, along with many family members and friends recommended books, song lyrics, Bible passages, etc. to comfort my broken heart.

My prayer partner Nisha and her husband Eld. Robertson blessed me too. Talking things out with them, my husband, daughter, Dad, my brothers, aunts, uncles, Godmother, cousins and friends helped some. Sometimes.

My cousin Nicole texted me hundreds of times, checking in and reminding me to eat, sleep and rest. Then, my good friend and dear sister Lecia empathetically walked with me every single step of the way, sharing with me great advice on dealing with my Mom's passing.

My Dad checked in on us every day, sometimes calling five times or more. So did some of my Mom's siblings and other relatives. We got word from my Aunt Georgia, Godmother Kathryn and friends on social media that church members were praying for our strength.

Interestingly, my brothers and I found it difficult and too emotional to talk to each other for any real length of time. In a strange way, the three of us avoided each other for some time...giving ourselves space and time to compartmentalize our Mom's life, legacy and impact.

I started walking on the treadmill for an hour at

my local gym. Thinking about the three generations I was blessed to meet, love, know and learn from, including two great-grandmothers, all four of my grandparents and my parents.

I found much solace going into Mom's room, lying on her bed, talking to her out loud as if she were still here, talking to her when I look at myself in the mirror, smelling her clothes and favorite perfumes, browsing through her photo albums, watching her favorite movies, listening to her favorite songs, reading her Bible, replaying her voicemails and videos ... and even wearing some of her clothes.

Doing all this helped me realize that Dr. Patricia Russell-McCloud is right when she says, "Every goodbye ain't gone."

DACKEYIA Q. STERLING

___Chapter 3___

___What I Didn't Do___
___When Mom Passed___

I started slowing everything down when Mom died. My life as an author was moving fast with the upcoming release of my 5th book, but I cleared my calendar and canceled engagements -- in an effort not to overload my emotions.

Throwing myself into work after experiencing Mom's real-life, in-your-face-now death seemed impossible. So, instead of business as usual, I decided to step back and take care of myself. I quickly started categorizing what was important.

What I didn't do was panic. I didn't stress out about work that wasn't getting done. I didn't tolerate *any* drama. I didn't listen to a lot of advice. I didn't trip on anything.

I also didn't recognize myself, or these new feelings. I didn't stay angry.

Chapter 4

Strength You Gain When Mom Dies

As reality of Mom's passing sinks in more and more, I realize that incredible strength to endure rises up each day. I consider every ounce of strength a great gift and blessing from God.

Before my Mom died, was I naive? A little. Was I arrogant? I see now, in retrospect, yes...and yes definitely. Why do I say that? Because, up until my Mother passed away, in my world as it had been, other people's Mom's died. Not mine. Not mine! No. Other people's Mom's passed away. I offered condolences. Felt sympathy. Prayed for them, thought about and sent cards or notes of support.

Well, now, after sitting on that front row in church, with my dear Mother laying at rest, with the classic gospel song *"Goin' Up Yonder"* playing as family and friends cried, filed by the casket and some kissing my Mother goodbye during that parting view, every virtue and character trait I have has been challenged and put to test.

Of course I didn't think my Mother would live forever. But, I never thought she would die either. And, never in a million years did I envision what life would be like without her. Was I super spoiled? Or, super blessed? I smile thinking it's a little of both!

I'm glad that I can smile again. I'm glad that I can move throughout most days now without crying like a big baby!

That's growth, strength and powerful. Trust me, if you're currently feeling melancholic, depressed, indifferent, pained, put upon, in denial, saddened beyond words, you will smile again too! It just takes time.

Chapter 5

The #1 Song on YouTube that Describes PERFECTLY How I Felt When My Mom Died

If you have time, scroll over to YouTube and listen closely to the lyrics to this song by the late gospel singer Marion Williams -- *"Standing Here Wondering (Which Way to Go)."* It's three minutes, 28 seconds (3:28) of power. If you're anything like me, you will find truth in these words.

Your Notes:

_____

_____

_____

_____

_____

_____

_____

_____

_____

_____

_____

_____

_____

_____

_____

_____

_____

_____

<u>*Chapter 6*</u>

12 Fears You Might Face When Mom Dies

Extreme Shock

Deep Grief

Overwhelming Sorrow

Inconsolable Tears

A Changing Reality

A New and Different You

A New Life

Healthy Healing Challenges

Lingering Regrets

Idle Time

Isolation

Loneliness

You can easily add more fears to this list. One of my greatest fears in the months after my Mom passed was that I would never genuinely smile again. Every time I took a picture, whether I was happy or sad, the sorrow in my eyes shone through like razors. I couldn't hide it. So, what did I do? I stopped taking photos for a while -- until one day I noticed a tiny sparkle returning to my eyes!

Remember this:

Adjusting to life after the loss of Mom is paramount. Whether we like it or not, time does not stand still. We must face our fears and redefine this new chapter of our lives!

Assignment:

1). Write a short list of 3 things you will do to conquer the fears you face.

2). Look in the mirror and smile. Your legacy is staring right at you!

<u>Chapter 7</u>

12 Simple Things You Can Do Right Now to Feel Better

Breathe

Cry

Eat

Rest

Exercise

Laugh

Pray

Write

Walk

Stare

Do nothing

Look at pictures

These simple, low-maintenance actions are power-packed! With the exception of eating, nothing on this list requires any money. And, they don't rely or depend on other people.

When you take focused time out of your day to do *any* of these 12 things -- and of course you can add your own healthy list of actions to this list, you will find yourself gaining ground.

I found more strength every time I did things on this list. By giving yourself permission to wind down and simplify this new season in your life, you will find yourself gaining more strength and clarity for the days ahead. The more time you spend releasing the grief, the more strength you gather to carry on. More time equals more strength.

<u>Chapter 8</u>

4 Real Ways to Get Immediate Support

Talk with family and friends

Fellowship with your church

Find a support group

Pray

<u>Support List</u>:

_____

_____

_____

_____

_____

_____

_____

_____

_____

_____

_____

_____

_____

_____

_____

_____

_____

Chapter 9

When You Are the Caregiver

*When you are the caregiver for your Mother,
and she passes away,
give yourself extra time to heal.*

During the eight years that I was primary caregiver for my Mother, I found it an honor to be my Mom's daughter, foot soldier and friend. Although she was chronically ill for a lengthy time, please understand and know that Mom was still trying to *"run the show"* as if she were 100% well. So much so that I now joke that "Mom had me on the run like I was Flo Jo!" (referring to the late Olympic Gold Medalist).

We bound together as a family and successfully handled this Herculean responsibility -- juggling medicine regimes, meal preparation and the long list of never-ending caregiving tasks -- like auto-pilots!

Helping take care of my Mother until the end is one of richest experiences of my life. I am grateful to God for giving my family and I the strength and provision to do it well.

I challenge and encourage all caregivers to stay laser-focused on rest and restoration at this time! Caregiving takes its toll on you. It is important to rebuild and move forward in life now, holding onto the great lessons, love, shared stories, family traditions, laughter, quality time and priceless gems you picked up from your Mother along the way.

Chapter 10

The #1 Way You Can Honor Your Mother's Life and Legacy

The secret I am about to share with you literally helped save my life! It is a piece of powerful advice that one of my childhood mentors, Mrs. Rhoda Dawson Wiley gave me about six months after my Mom passed. I was searching and searching and searching for outlets to relieve the pain in my heart, the pounding headaches that wouldn't go away.

As I rummaged through boxes in storage going through Mom's things, looking for nothing in particular, I stumbled across one of my old boxes. Inside was a 21-year-old letter addressed to me from Mrs. Wiley. I emailed Mrs. Wiley and she called me early the next morning. When I shared with her the struggle I was having adjusting to life without my Mother, Mrs. Wiley dropped a pearl of wisdom that touched me deeply -- sharing from her heart how she pulled herself together when her dear Mother passed years earlier. She told me exactly what I needed to do -- and ultimately changed the trajectory of my world.

Here it is: the #1 way you can honor your Mother's life is to pull yourself together, fix yourself up and LIVE the absolute best life you can!

Take a deep breath and let that sink it. Pull yourself together. If that means talking to yourself in the mirror out loud and literally saying, "Let's get it together!" Fix yourself up! No more t-shirts and sweats day in and day out. No more ponytails everyday. No more barely making it to school, work, the gym, church. Beautify yourself. Dress to the nines, upgrade your wardrobe, empower your mind, embrace your strengths and LIVE!

Remember this:

The #1 way to honor and celebrate your Mother's life is by living the BEST life you can!

Assignment:

1). Write a short list of 3 things you will do to honor your Mom's life and legacy.

2). Look in the mirror and smile. Your legacy is staring right at you!

<u>*Ways I Will Honor My Mother:*</u>

_____

_____

_____

_____

_____

_____

_____

_____

_____

_____

_____

_____

_____

_____

_____

_____

_____

Chapter 11

Don't Be Surprised ...

...If you find yourself angry, shocked or in disbelief that your Mom has died.

...If you overhear others talking about their Mother's more than ever before.

...If you find yourself crying big, crocodile tears for no reason, on any given day.

...If you go on unplanned shopping sprees. Smile! Retail therapy can be good for you. Just don't go overboard like I did.

...If your concentration is off.

...If your inspiration wanes.

...If things fall apart. It's only temporary. Nothing stays the same forever.

...If you start SEEING people for the first time in a long time.

...If certain family and friends don't call you. I've learned that while many may not know what to say, others simply do not care. The truth hurts sometimes but try not to take it too personal. Make notes and keep LIVING and honoring yourself.

...If you find yourself in bed, with the covers pulled over your head, balled up in the fetal position crying when you should be somewhere doing something else more important. Grieving takes time.

...If you let every phone call go to voicemail and every doorbell ring go unanswered. Sometimes you simply can't or don't want to talk.

...If you make mistakes during this time.

Remember this:

Your life just changed forever. You are entitled to whatever time it takes to heal.

Assignment:

Be more careful!

*I accidentally burned my hand and arm while cooking shortly after my Mom's passing. Mind you, I

have been cooking for almost 30 years and NEVER burned myself before. I wish someone had shared this gem with me.

DACKEYIA Q. STERLING

<u>*Chapter 12*</u>

Good Advice to Remember

"God is in the renewing and reviving business."

~ Mrs. Rhoda Wiley

Advice to Remember:

_____

_____

_____

_____

_____

_____

_____

_____

_____

_____

_____

_____

_____

_____

_____

_____

Chapter 13

The "Power to Live" Song on YouTube That Helped Save My Life

I stopped crying everyday exactly 10 months and one day after my Mother passed. Finally, after many prayers, questions, tear-soaked pillows, face towels, handkerchiefs and napkins, I got my breakthrough!

Where and how did I get my breakthrough, strength and power to write this book in a week? For months on end after Mom passed I would find myself up late into the midnight hour scrolling through video after video looking for inspiration. Then, the Lord touched me and I found my help! There are several versions of this same song led by Pastor Kervy Brown on YouTube...but the *"Power to Live"* song that helped snatch me out of the pit of despair and into the hope of a new and different life is 9 minutes,

6 seconds long (9:06).

I don't know this man, have never been to his church. But, I have watched this video at least 20 times. When you're ready, take a peek at this song on YouTube. **Here it is**:

https://www.youtube.com/watch?v=CDC1fgPcAZY

<u>Chapter 14</u>

Powerful Scriptures to Reference

I found it incredibly hard to focus on anything for any length of time when my Mom passed away. However, I did find reading and reciting certain Scriptures in the Bible soothing to a degree. About a year before the inevitable, my cousin Jondell sent me three encouraging Post-It notes in the mail with the following passages hand-written on them:

<u>Matthew 11:28-30 (KJV)</u>
28 Come unto me, all ye that labour and are heavy laden, and I will give you rest.

29 Take my yoke upon you, and learn of me; for I am meek and lowly in heart: and ye shall find rest unto your souls.

30 For my yoke is easy, and my burden is light.

For many months prior to my Mom's death, I would recite these lines over and over again.

Then, following my Mom's passing, I looked these and many others up on my own:

Psalms 27:14 (KJV)
Wait on the Lord: be of good courage, and he shall strengthen thine heart: wait, I say, on the Lord.

Psalms 46: 1 (KJV)
God is our refuge and strength, a very present help in trouble.

Isaiah 40:30-31 (KJV)
Even the youths shall faint and be weary, and the young men shall utterly fall: But they that wait upon the Lord shall renew their strength; they shall mount up with wings as eagles; they shall run, and not be weary; and they shall walk, and not faint.

**I really got hung up on the "wait on the Lord" part. So much so that when people asked me *"how are you doing?"* I would reply, *"I'm waiting on the Lord to renew my strength."*

***Note**: All Scriptures referenced are from the King James Version of the Holy Bible.*

<u>*Chapter 15*</u>

Helpful Resources to Consider

Grief Share - <u>*www.griefshare.org*</u> - Grief Recovery Support

<u>*How to Survive to Loss of a Loved*</u> by Melba Colgrove, Ph.D., Harold H. Bloomfield, M.D. & Peter McWilliams

<u>*The Funeral Is Just the Beginning: Everything You Need to Do When a Loved One Dies*</u> by Amy Levine

__Note__: Since this is a quick-read book, I list the three above that I personally discovered. A quick internet search will reveal millions of bereavement and grief resources available today.

Check with your local hospital and listings in your local phone book for more resources near you.

More Resources:

_____

_____

_____

_____

_____

_____

_____

_____

_____

_____

_____

_____

_____

_____

_____

_____

_____

<u>*Chapter 16*</u>

31 Ideas to Encourage Your Healing Heart

Keep this quick list close as a "go-to" reminder of things you can do!

1. Create photo and video albums of your Mom.
2. Honor your Mother's final wishes.
3. Take a bath.
4. Take a nap.
5. Take a walk.
6. Paint a room.
7. Create scrapbooks of your Mother's life.
8. Play the piano. *I find it extremely relaxing!
9. Listen to good music.
10. Go for long drives.
11. Eat gourmet.
12. Do something new.
13. Create a bucket list.
14. Go on vacation.
15. Get glammed up
16. Change your atmosphere.
17. Write in your journal.
18. Write a book.
19. Sing.

20. Dance.
21. Spend time with elderly family members.
22. Spend time with babies.
23. Donate items to charity.
24. Share heirlooms.
25. Share stories.
26. Compile your Mother's recipes into a cookbook.
27. Create a blog.
28. Be honest about your emotions.
29. Keep handkerchiefs and tissue close by.
30. Get healthier.
31. Be encouraged!

<u>The Wrap Up</u>

Joy Will Rise Again...and Again

It may be hard to fathom right now, but just as sure as Winter turns to Spring and night turns into day, joy will return to your life after your Mom dies. I NEVER in a million years thought I would be able to experience this truth. Yet, here on these pages I have shared a few lessons from my heart.

It is my prayer that you will find all the strength you need to square your shoulders back, hold your head up high and LIVE victoriously. I know that is what my Mother taught and wants me to do...and that is *exactly* what I will do!

<u>*Say it with me*</u>:

"I will honor and celebrate my Mother's life by living the BEST life I can!"

10 Great Memories of My Mother:

_____

_____

_____

_____

_____

_____

_____

_____

_____

_____

_____

_____

_____

_____

_____

_____

Special Acknowledgments
✳✳✳

I am grateful to God for giving me strength to endure, and for all the calls, visits, advice, prayers, gifts, flowers, candy, love and support, during this time of bereavement, change, loss, growth and life.

I acknowledge, thank and appreciate all my family and friends -- and want to take this moment to especially thank you: Queency Abad, the Abrams Family (Janice, Betty Jean, Joann, Cliff and Raianne & Cousins), Eddie and Rose Abrams, Dr. Noman Absar, Gayle Adams, Lori Adams, Willie B. and MaryAnn Adkins, the Anthony Family, Mary Arnold, Amy Allison, Maxi Anderson, Susiette Anderson, Aunt Georgia Mae Bass, Nona Cohen-Bowman, Terris and Barbara Bynum, Calvary Community Church, Pamela Cathion Carr, Dr. Holly Carter, Sis. Louise Coleman, Uncle Algie Craft, Aunt Clota Mae Craft, Aunt Violene Craft, Monique Causey Crowley, Alan

Davis, Bertha Davis, Floredia Davis, Dr. Gerri Davis, Jahmal Davis Family (Jahmal, Astasha, Daniel, Nia and Josiah), Thomas Davis, Sr., Thomas Davis, Jr., Victor DeCuir, Linda Demery, Gertrude Dickson, Dennis & Cherita Dilley & Sons, Steve and Alaire Dippel, Ardelia Dorsey, Clency and Brenda Easterling, Debra Easterling, Donald and Tena Easterling, Jamal Easterling, Percy and Cynthia Easterling, Percy Easterling, Jr. (Lil' Perc), Vivian Evans, Komeka Freeman, Auntie Winnie French, Deanna Garcia, Adia Griffith, Okpara Griffith, Gilda Hammond, Aunt Emma Lee Harper, Pastor Lloyd Harrison and First Lady Bobette Jamison-Harrison, Howard University, Sonja Inge, Keyandra Jefferson, George Johnson, Kelvin and Cheryl Johnson, the entire Johnson Family, Catherine Jones, Kaiser Unit at St. Agnes Hospital, Professor Vera J. Katz, Aunt Ida Mae Killingsworth, Thomas Kourth, Dr. Judi Moore Latta, Ronald and Victoria Lawson, Matthew and Kim Leeke, Carlton and Bobbi Mack, Georgia McCarver, Maurice and Nicole McCarver (Lil' Reece, Quez, Nia and Lyric), Michelle McCarver, Pastor J.W.

McCoy, Cousin Annie McDonald, Marion McDowell, Aunt Roberta McLean, Carmen Davenporte McNeal, Tondra TaJuan Mercer, Wanda Mercer, Bobbi Merrill, Anthony Monroe, Deaundria "DeDe" Moore, Pat Mosby, Jason Moulton, Nate and Gloria Oliver, Trina Chandler Orme, Alisca Redmon, Aunt Elizabeth Reese, Willie Ray Reese, Dorothy Roberts, C.A. and Barbara Robertson, Pastor Larry Robertson and First Lady Nisha Robertson, Pastor Hanson Rogers and First Lady Kathryn Rogers (my Godparents), Dr. Luis Ruiz, the Shields Family (Larry, Melissa, CJ, Jazmin and Joshua), Glenda Simmons, Megan Simmons, Yvette Smith, Shawn Solomon, Chad Sterling, DeLayna Sterling, Jondell Taylor, Kedra Taylor, Tawanna McFarland Taylor, Pastor Charles Thomas and First Lady Pauline Thomas, Dwayne Thompson, Kimberley Thompson, the Video Ministry at Greater Mt. Calvary Holy Church in D.C., Anthony Waldren and the Starvin' Artist Family & Crew (Kim, Kayla, Ava, Cameron, Gbenga and Stephen), Rickie and Tiphany Weeks, Rhoda Dawson Wiley, Professor Sonja Williams, Elder David Winn, Bishop Robert

Winn and Sis. Mattie Winn & Family, and last but certainly not least, my fabulous aunt and friend Anne M. Woods.

Much, much love to my family and friends all over the world -- with extra love to my California, Mississippi, Florida, Texas and New York relatives!

Antracia Moorings and Lecia J. Rives Salaam, thank you for your steadfastness, patience and love. From your own reservoir of experiences, you really helped walk me through!

To everyone reading this book, I bid you more strength to endure, more power to love and greater inspiration to LIVE big!

About the Author
***

Dackeyia Q. Sterling is the CEO/Publisher of numerous nonfiction titles. Her trademark *Entertainment Power Players® Directory*, recommended by the American Library Association's *Choice Magazine*, is known throughout the entertainment, educational and publishing arenas as one of the best entertainment career resource books featuring more than 5,000 contacts in Fashion, Film, Music, Sports, TV and Video Gaming.

A native of Vallejo, CA, Sterling is an alumna of Howard University in Washington, D.C. She is a tireless researcher who enjoys motivational speaking and mentoring emerging talent. She is a former Hollywood literary agent and talent manager whose speaking invitations include Hampton University, Harvard University, Howard University, Penn State

University, the University of Memphis and the University of Southern California (USC), to name a few. She is a loving wife, nurturing Mom and an avid sock collector.

To contact Sterling directly for interviews or engagements, email CEO@EntertainmentPower.com.

***